Beginning BLUES GUITAR
RHYTHM and SOLOS

Taught by Al Ek

Text by Steve Gorenberg
DVD presentation by Al Ek
ISBN 978-1-60378-376-7

Copyright © 2011 Cherry Lane Music Company
International Copyright Secured   All Rights Reserved

The music, text, design and graphics in this publication are protected by copyright law. Any duplication or transmission, by any means, electronic, mechanical, photocopying, recording or otherwise, is an infringement of copyright.

Visit our website at www.cherrylaneprint.com

Contents

Introduction 3
About the Author 3
Blues Basics 4
    The Chromatic Scale 4
    The Major Scale 5
    The Major Pentatonic Scale 5
    The Minor Pentatonic Scale 6
    Counting the Beat 7
    Guitar Techniques 8
The Shuffle Groove 10
    The Shuffle Groove Rhythm 10
    The Shuffle Groove Rhythm with a Quick Change 11
    The Shuffle Groove Solo 12
The Rock 'n' Roll Groove 13
    The Rock 'n' Roll Groove Rhythm 13
    The Rock 'n' Roll Groove Solo 14
The Mojo Groove 15
    The Mojo Groove Rhythm 15
    The Mojo Groove Solo 16
    The Shuffle and Rock 'n' Roll Solos Transposed to C 17
    The Mojo Solo Transposed to A 19
The Slow Blues Groove 20
    The Slow Blues Groove Rhythm 20
    The Slow Blues Groove Solo 21
    The Slow Blues Groove Solo II 22
The Boogaloo Groove 24
    The Boogaloo Groove Rhythm 24
    The Boogaloo Groove Solo 25
    The Rock 'n' Roll and Mojo Solos Transposed to E 26
    The Shuffle Solo Transposed to E 28
The Backwards Shuffle 29
    The Backwards Shuffle Rhythm 29
    The Backwards Shuffle Solo 30

Jam Tracks: On DVD only; see Main Menu.

Introduction

Al Ek teaches six different rhythm parts, each with its own solo, and shows you how each solo can work over different rhythm grooves and keys. Each rhythm part and solo is included in the book. Designed for the beginning blues guitarist, everything on the DVD is played up to speed and then broken down note by note. Jam tracks for each style are included on the DVD.

About the Author

Musician, performer, bandleader, teacher, and guitarist Al Ek has been a mainstay on the Las Vegas music scene for years. His career started over 30 years ago when he was playing harmonica in Milwaukee and Chicago blues clubs. He later played in the Shuffle-Aires and opened for such legendary blues and roots acts as Johnny Winter, Fabulous Thunderbirds, Los Lobos, Lonnie Brooks, and NRBQ, among others. In 1992 he accepted an offer to play in the "American Superstar" show at the famous Las Vegas Flamingo. He has since recorded numerous sessions for various Las Vegas artists as well as radio and television spots. Ek currently teaches at A.J.'s Music, is guitarist for the House of Blues Schoolhouse Band, and plays and tours with the Pete Contino Band.

Blues Basics

Let's begin with an introduction to some of the basic scales and techniques we'll be using throughout the program. Take some time to familiarize yourself with the terminology and musical symbols in this section.

The Chromatic Scale

There are a total of twelve different notes in the chromatic scale, including all of the *natural notes* (the letters of the musical alphabet, A through G), in addition to the *sharps* and *flats* (the notes in between the natural notes). On the guitar, the distance (in pitch) from one fret to the next on the same string is called a *half step*. The distance of two frets is called a *whole step*. Playing all twelve consecutive half steps in ascending or descending order creates one *octave* of the chromatic scale. An octave is the distance (in pitch) from any note name, for example E, to the next higher or lower E in the musical alphabet.

The example below shows the notes of the chromatic scale on the low E string (6th string), ascending and descending. The note names are indicated above the notation staff. The sharp (♯) next to a note raises its pitch by a half step; the flat (♭) next to a note lowers its pitch by a half step. When playing the scale in ascending order, sharps are used. When playing the scale in descending order, flats are used. Learning the chromatic scale will help you to learn the notes on the guitar and find your way up and down the fretboard.

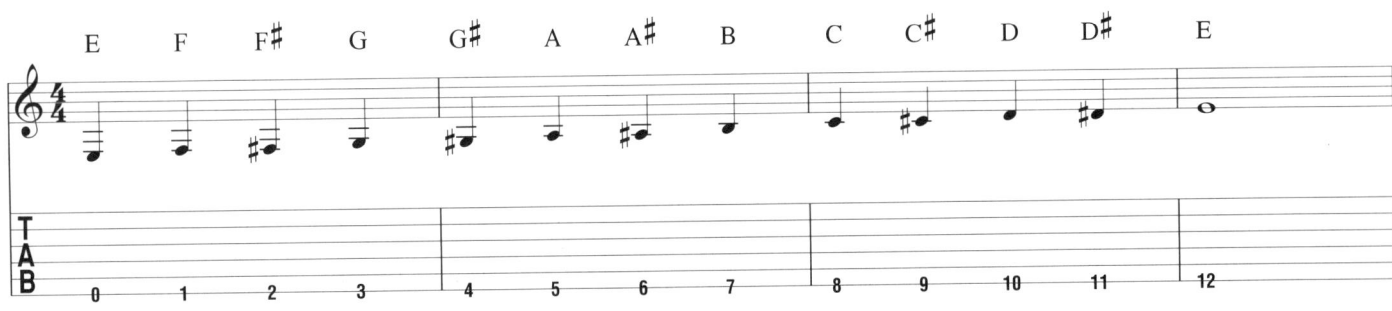

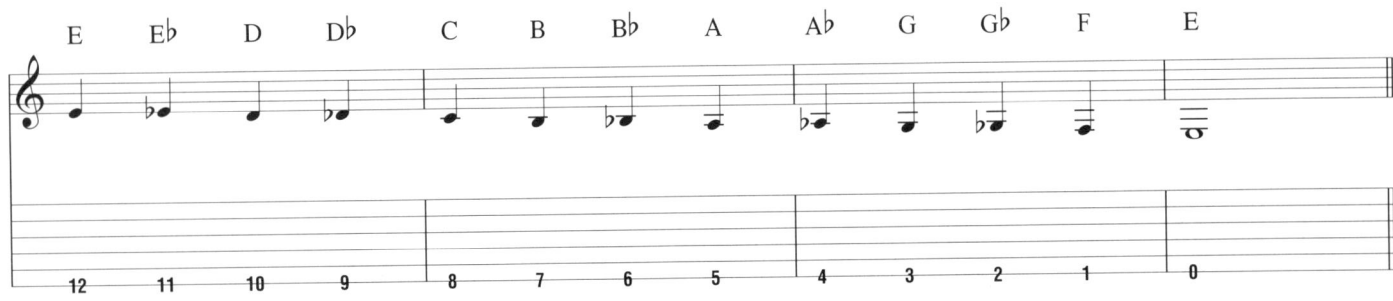

The Major Scale

Now let's move on to one of the most common scales in music. The major scale is a seven-note scale that's made up of a series of whole steps and half steps, going up the musical alphabet letter by letter. The most basic major scale is the C major scale because it contains no sharps or flats. Every other major key utilizes sharps or flats to achieve the proper series of whole steps and half steps needed to create the major scale.

The example below shows one octave of the A major scale. The note names are indicated above the notation, and the proper left hand fingering is indicated below the tab staff.

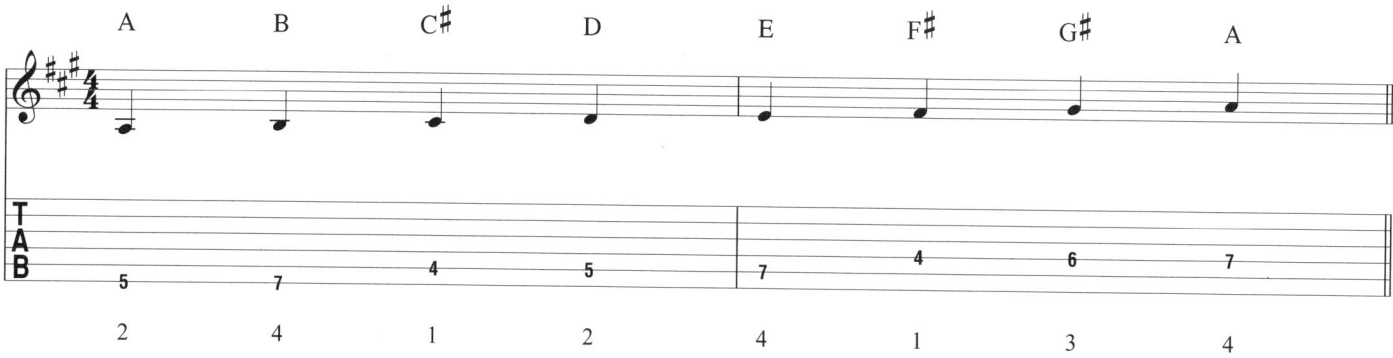

The steps of the major scale are often referred to by number using roman numerals. Each of these scale steps has a chord that's constructed on it, making up all of the standard chords in this key. In the chart below, the upper case numerals refer to major chords, and the lower case numerals refer to minor chords and diminshed chords. The first step of the scale is also referred to as the *tonic*, though some people call it the *root note*; in this key, the tonic is A. For all major keys, the I, IV and V chords are major chords. These three chords form the basis of many blues songs.

The Major Pentatonic Scale

The major pentatonic scale is an abbreviated version of the regular major scale. By removing the 4th and 7th steps of the major scale, we're left with the five-note major pentatonic scale.

Now let's take the A major pentatonic scale and play it one octave higher.

By putting both octaves of the scale together, we get the full, two-octave major pentatonic scale.

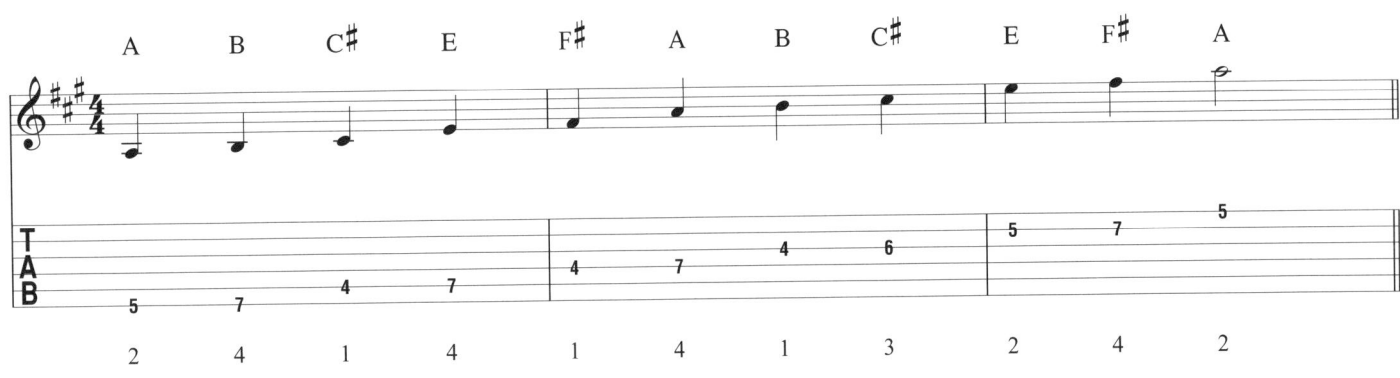

The Minor Pentatonic Scale

There's also a minor version of the pentatonic scale. The two-octave A minor pentatonic scale is shown in the following example. Memorize and practice this scale; the minor pentatonic scale is the most popular scale used in blues solos.

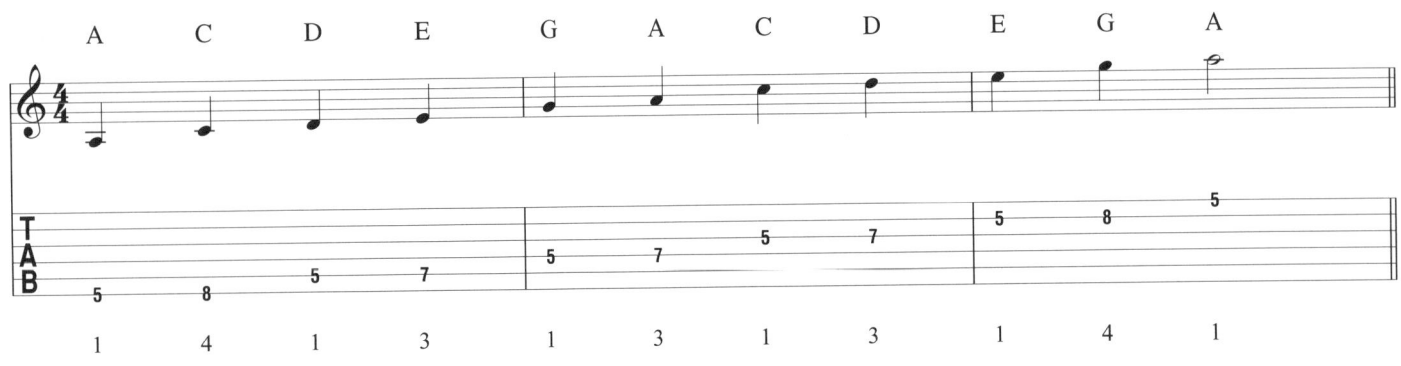

Counting the Beat

In most popular rock and blues, music is divided up into *measures* or groups of four beats. This is known as *4/4 time*, meaning four quarter notes per measure, with the quarter note counting as one beat. When a band counts off "One, two, three, four" at the beginning of a song, it represents one complete measure of music. Different types of note values are held for different durations within a measure. The chart below shows the different note values and how to count them.

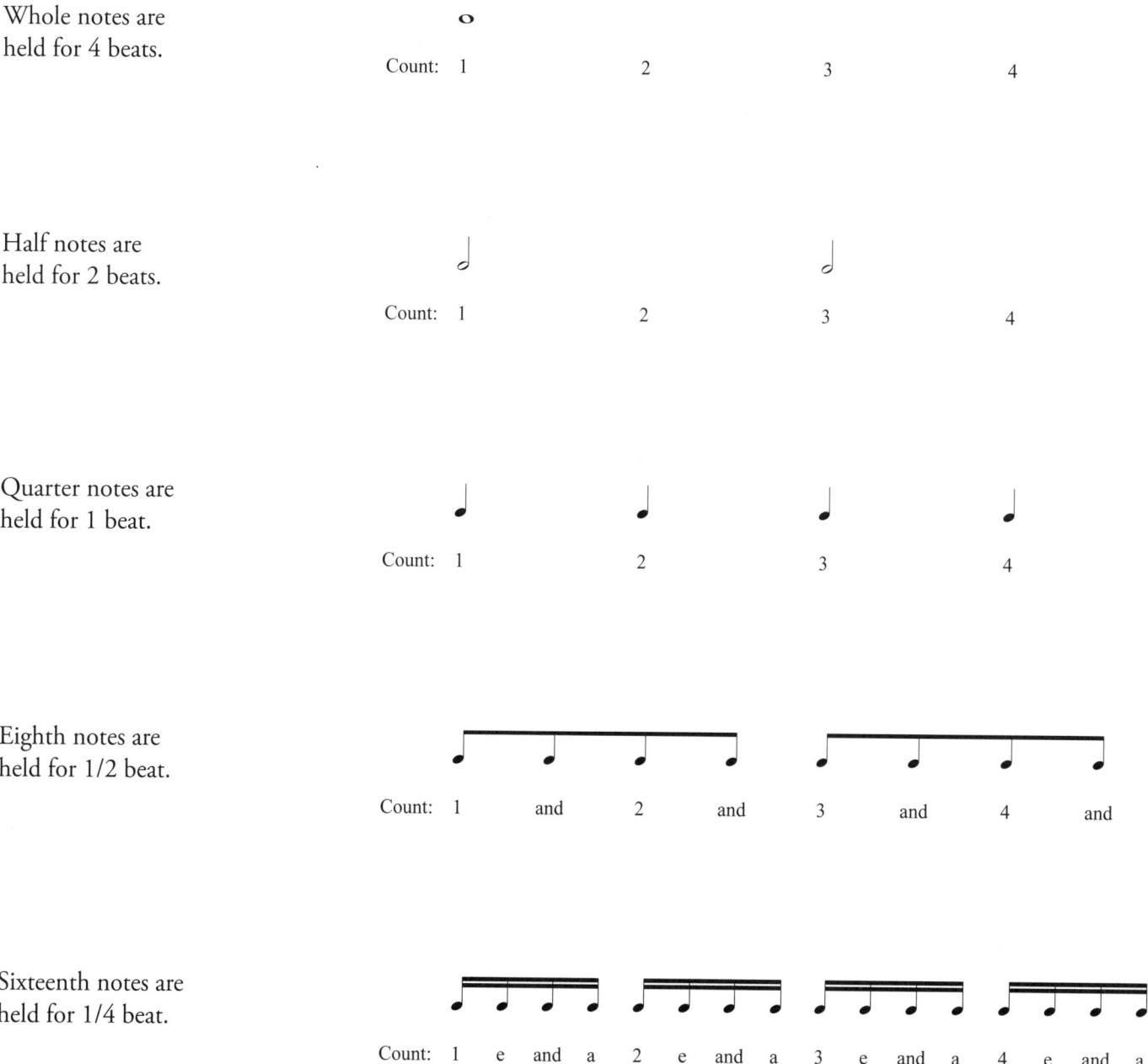

Guitar Techniques

Let's conclude this section by taking a look at some of the guitar techniques used to play solos. The following examples explore the different variations of these techniques, and show how they're depicted in music notation and tab.

Bends are a useful way to add expression to your playing. Bending a note involves holding down a fretted note and pushing upward (or sometimes downward) on the string to alter the pitch. There are several different types of bending techniques shown below that you should become familiar with.

HALF-STEP BEND:
Strike the note and bend up 1/2 step.

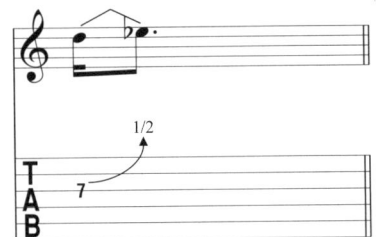

WHOLE-STEP BEND:
Strike the note and bend up one step.

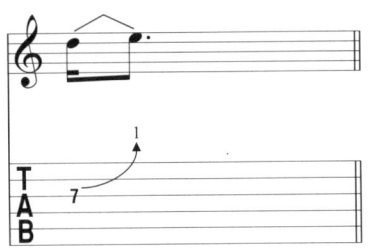

GRACE NOTE BEND:
Strike the note and immediately bend up as indicated.

SLIGHT (MICROTONE) BEND:
Strike the note and bend up 1/4 step.

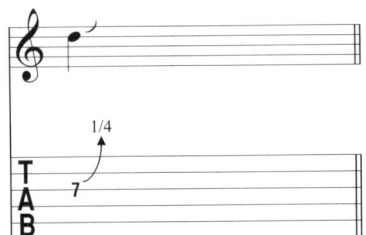

BEND AND RELEASE:
Strike the note and bend up as indicated, then release back to the original note. Only the first note is struck.

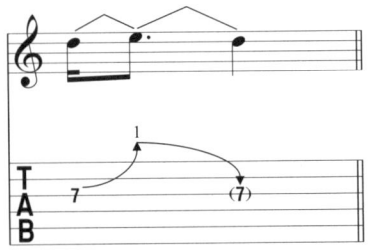

PRE-BEND:
Bend the note as indicated, then strike it.

Hammer-ons and pull-offs are performed by striking only the first of a series of notes, then allowing your left hand fingers to sound out the rest of the notes by pressing down or releasing them on the fretboard without picking. Both techniques can be used in combination to achieve a smooth, legato effect.

HAMMER-ON:
Strike the first (lower) note with one finger, then sound the higher note (on the same string) with another finger by fretting it without picking

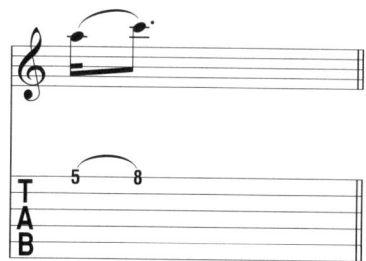

PULL-OFF:
Place both fingers on the notes to be sounded. Strike the first note and without picking, pull the finger off to sound the second (lower) note.

Slides are indicated using a diagonal line showing the direction of the slide (up or down in pitch along the neck). Continue pressing down on the fretboard as you slide from note to note.

LEGATO SLIDE:
Strike the first note and then slide the same fret-hand finger up or down to the second note. The second note is not struck.

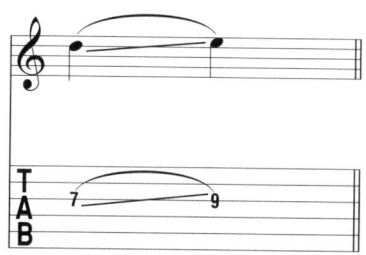

SHIFT SLIDE:
Same as legato slide, except the second note is struck.

Vibrato is the small, fast shaking of a sustained note with your left-hand finger. Vibrato also can be applied to a bent note.

VIBRATO:
The string is vibrated by rapidly bending and releasing the note with a left-hand finger.

WIDE VIBRATO:
The pitch is varied to a greater degree by vibrating with a left-hand finger.

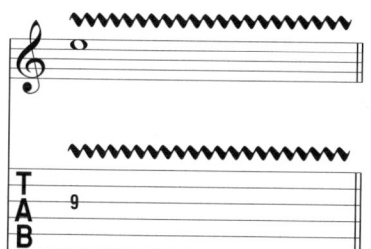

The Shuffle Groove

The Shuffle Groove Rhythm

Our first example is a basic blues shuffle in the key of A. To achieve the shuffle rhythm, the second eighth note of each beat (the upbeat) should lag a little to create an uneven, loping feel. Shuffle rhythm is a much easier concept to understand by hearing it. Listen to the backing track, count along, and try to get the shuffle feel in your head. Many blues standards, fast or slow, utilize the shuffle feel. The following rhythm is a standard I-IV-V *chord progression*, or a pattern or series of chords. This chord progression is also referred to as *12-bar blues*, a blues progression consisting of twelve bars (measures) of music. Our example below is the 12-bar blues in its simplest form. The A chord is the I chord, the D is the IV chord, and the E is the V chord.

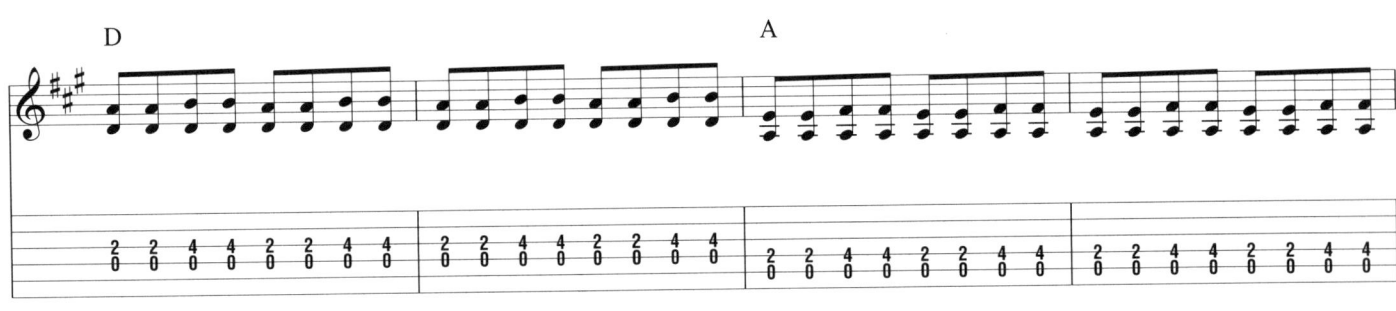

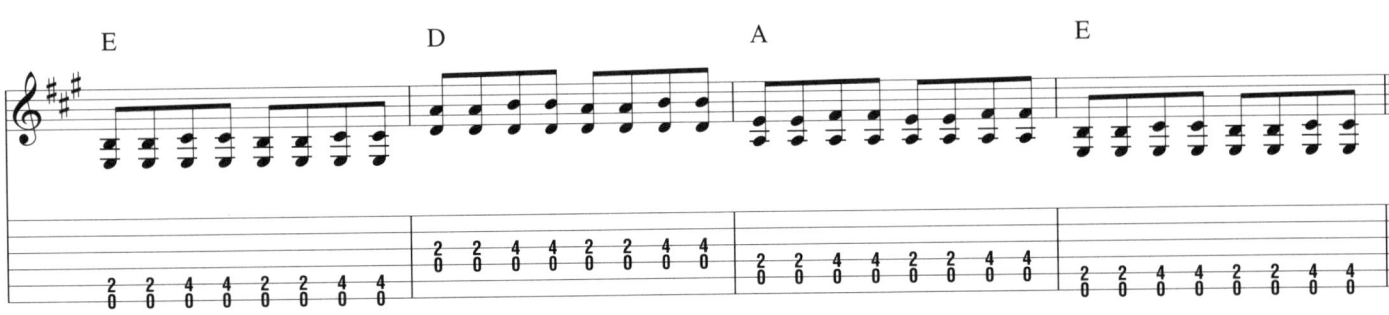

The Shuffle Groove Rhythm with a Quick Change

Now let's take the same chord progression and add a simple variation. For the second measure of the progression, play the IV chord (D) and then go back to the I chord (A) for the third measure, then play the rest of the progression the same as in the previous example. This common variation within the 12-bar blues is called a *quick change*. The jam track for this chapter on the accompanying DVD uses a quick change, shown in the example below.

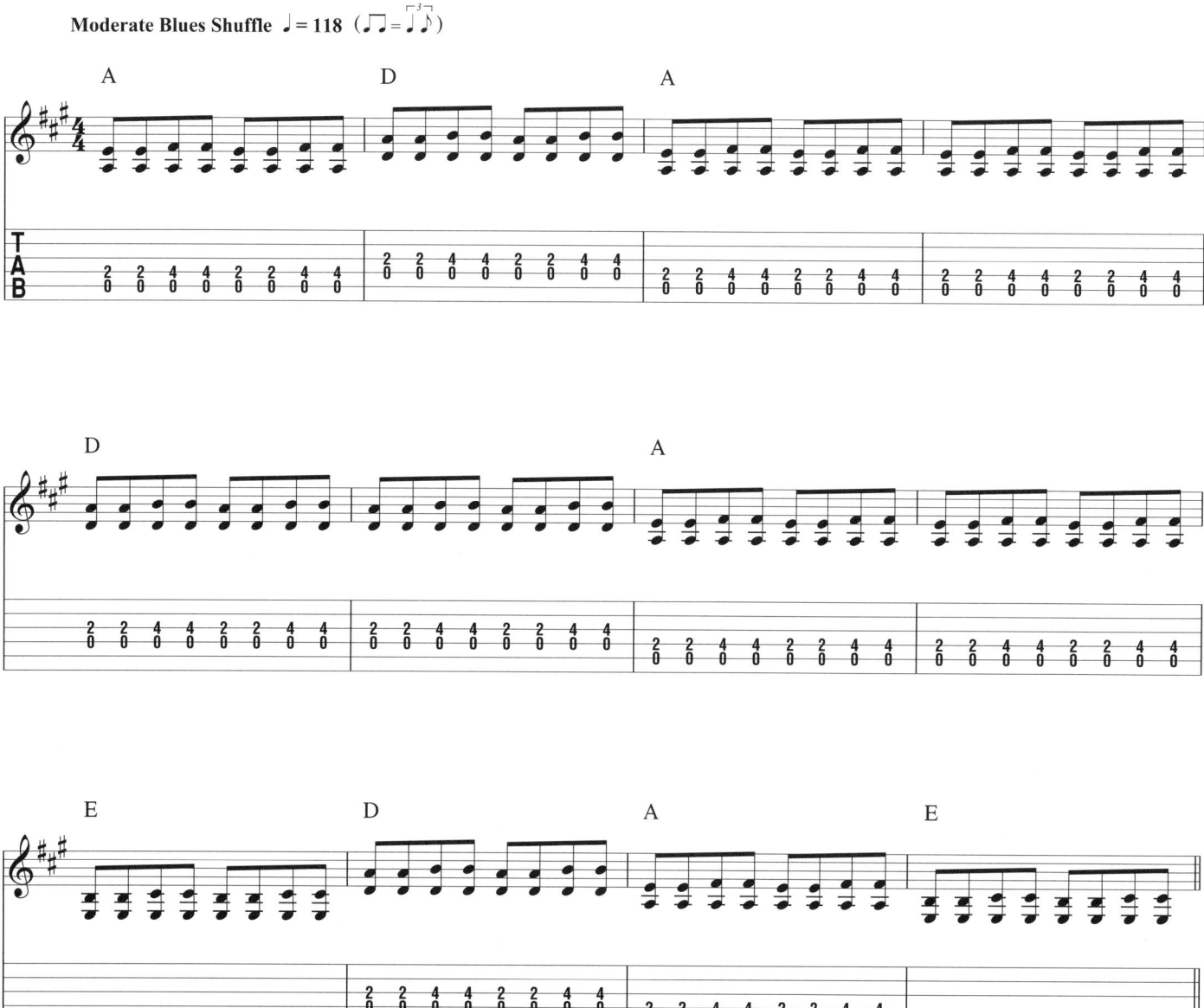

The Shuffle Groove Solo

Let's put a solo to the rhythm we just learned. The example below is based on the A minor pentatonic scale and incorporates some quarter step bends. The last few measures of the 12-bar blues are called the *turnaround* because they set up the progression to lead back to the beginning and repeat itself. The turnaround riff in the eleventh measure uses chromatic double stops, which should be played by plucking the lower notes with the pick and the higher notes with your ring finger.

The Rock 'n' Roll Groove

The Rock 'n' Roll Groove Rhythm

Our next rhythm is a standard rock groove using the same 12-bar blues progression from the previous chapter. The riff is similar to the one used for the Shuffle Groove Rhythm, but it's played at a faster tempo using *straight eighths*, without the shuffle feel.

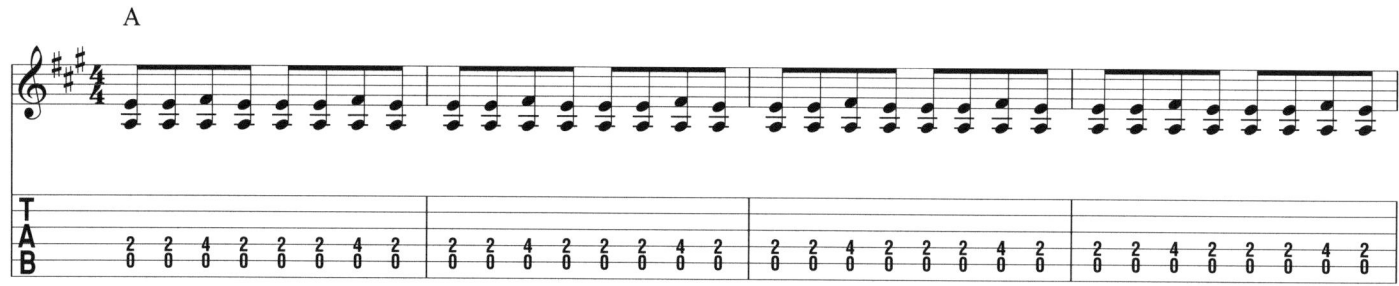

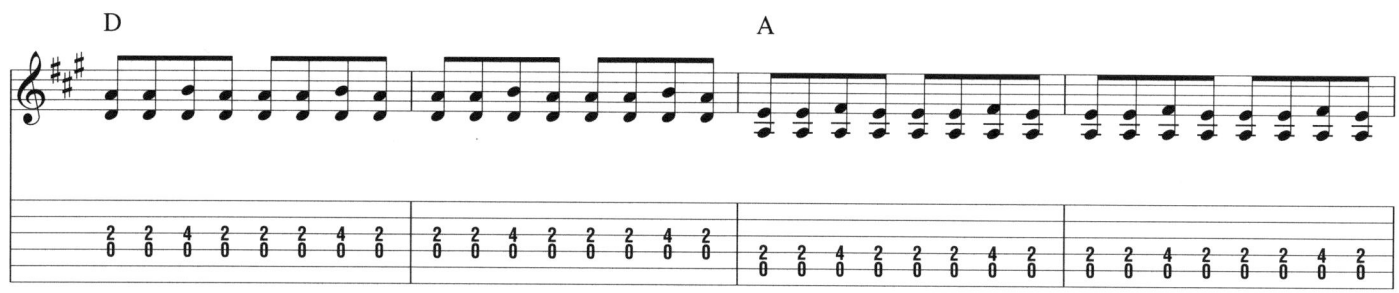

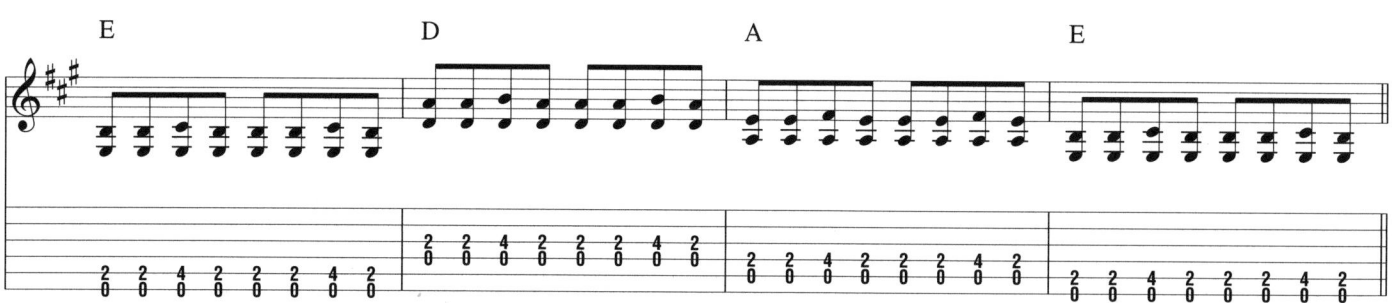

The Rock 'n' Roll Groove Solo

This next solo is a little more difficult and incorporates some additional lead techniques, including slides, hammer-ons and bends. Since this rhythm is in the same key as the Shuffle Groove, you can also play the Shuffle Groove Solo over it using a straight eighth feel. Then try playing the Rock 'n' Roll Solo over the Shuffle Groove jam track. The chord progression is the same for both examples; the only differences are the tempo and the feel.

The Mojo Groove

The Mojo Groove Rhythm

Now let's try a new rhythm in the key of C. The chord progression is almost the same as the previous 12-bar blues examples, but it uses all seventh chords and a slight variation in the tenth measure, where the V chord continues instead of moving to the IV chord.

The Mojo Groove Solo

Try the following solo over the Mojo Groove Rhythm. This lead uses a combination of the major and minor pentatonic scales and contains some tasteful question-and-answer phrasing in the melodies.

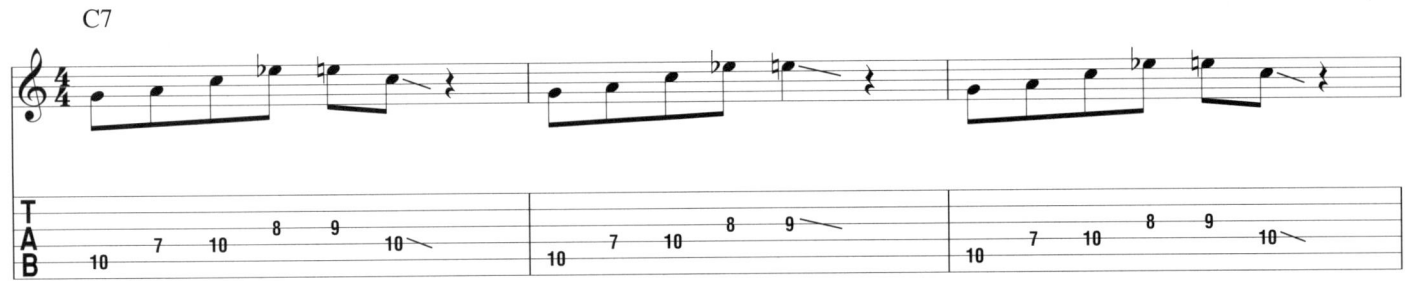

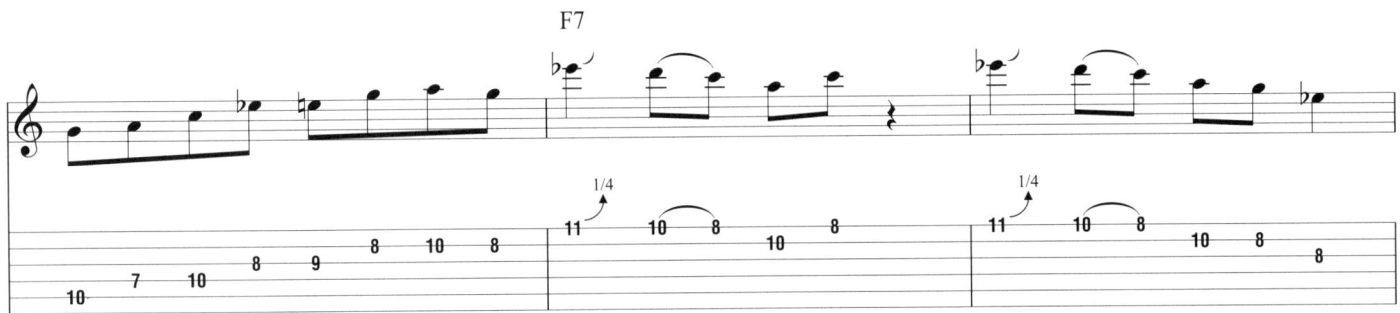

The Shuffle and Rock 'n' Roll Solos Transposed to C

Let's take the first two solos we learned in the key of A and *transpose* them to the key of C so they can be played over the Mojo Groove Rhythm. A piece of music is transposed by moving it note for note from one key to another. In this case, we simply need to move the solos three frets higher on the guitar. All of the riffs in the following solo should look familiar; the fingerings are virtually identical to the ones used in the previous chapters.

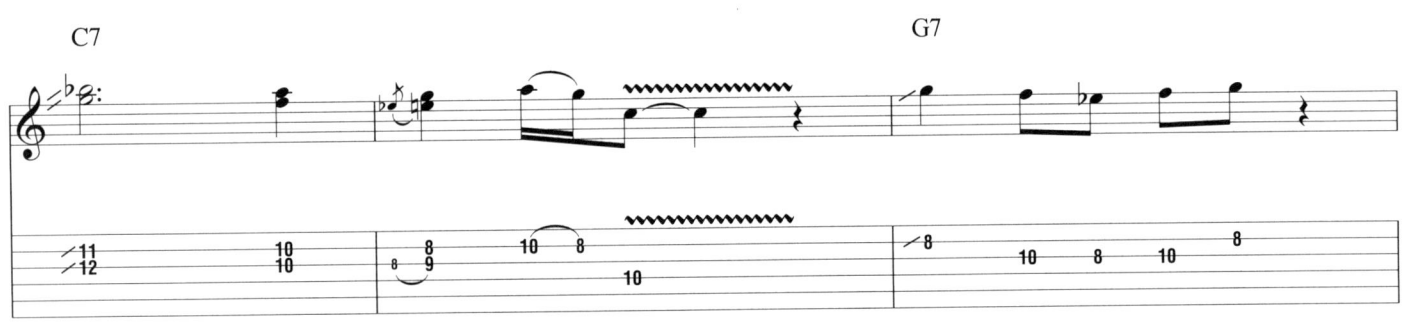

The Mojo Solo Transposed to A

We can also take the Mojo solo and play it over the Shuffle and Rock 'n' Roll Grooves. All you need to do is transpose the Mojo solo down three frets on the guitar to the key of A. We've made a slight change in the second measure and incorporated a quarter step bend, which fits well over the IV chord quick change used in this rhythm.

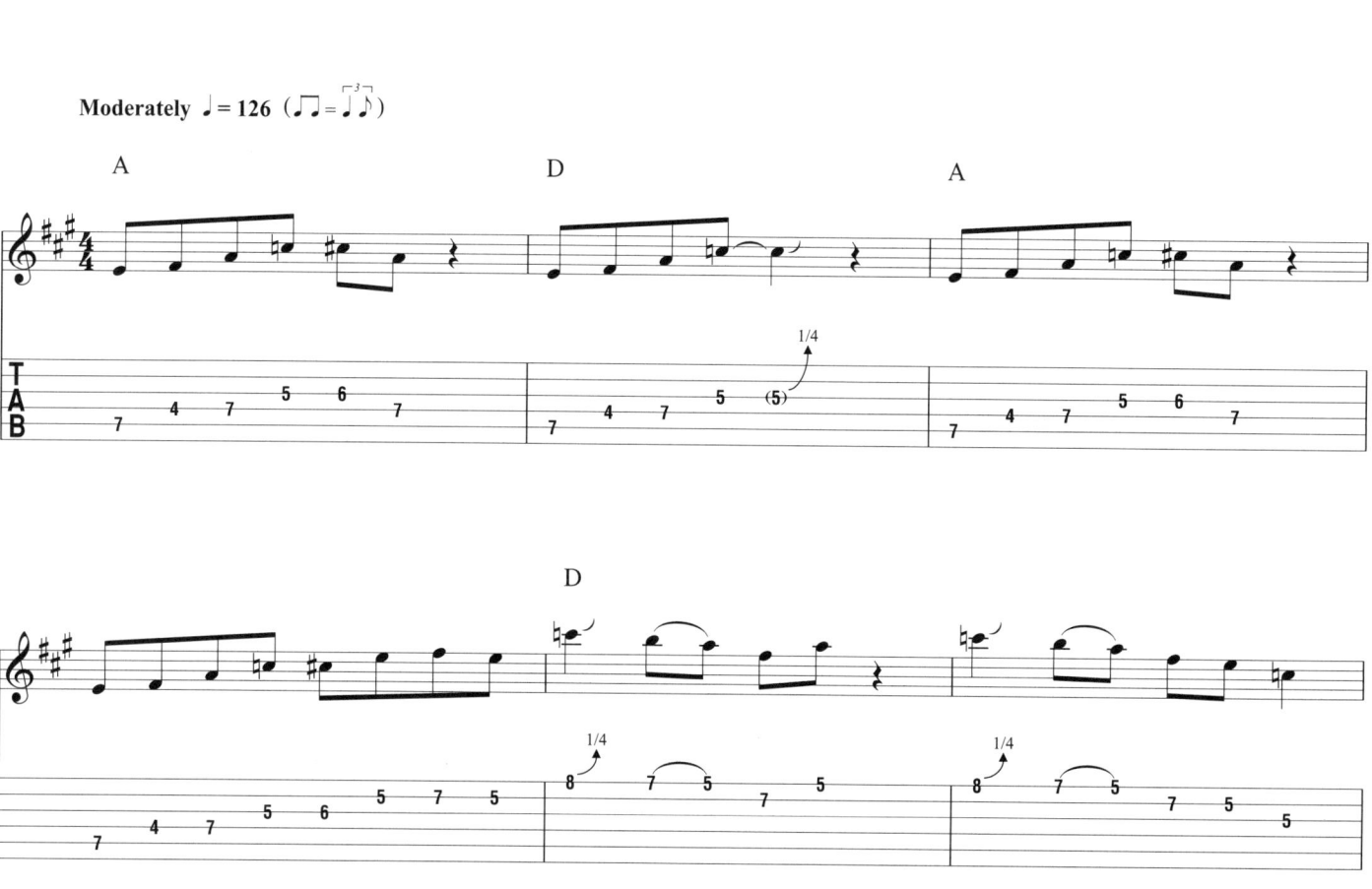

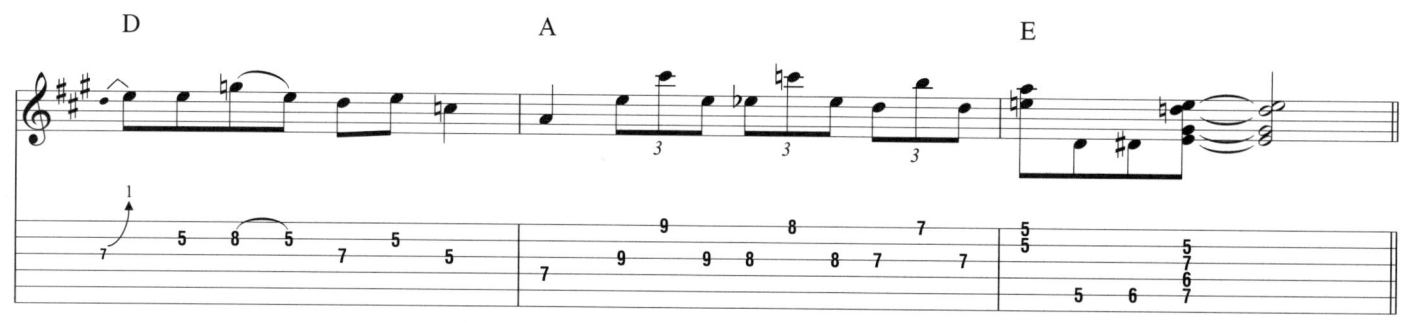

The Slow Blues Groove

The Slow Blues Groove Rhythm

This lesson covers one of the most popular variations of the 12-bar blues. The Slow Blues relies heavily on feel and uses a very slow shuffle rhythm. The following progression in the key of G is based on a I-IV-V with a quick change, and uses standard versions of 9th chords throughout. The chord symbols above the notation staff outline the basic progression. For the last measure of the turnaround, we've used G major and D7 chords to switch it up a bit.

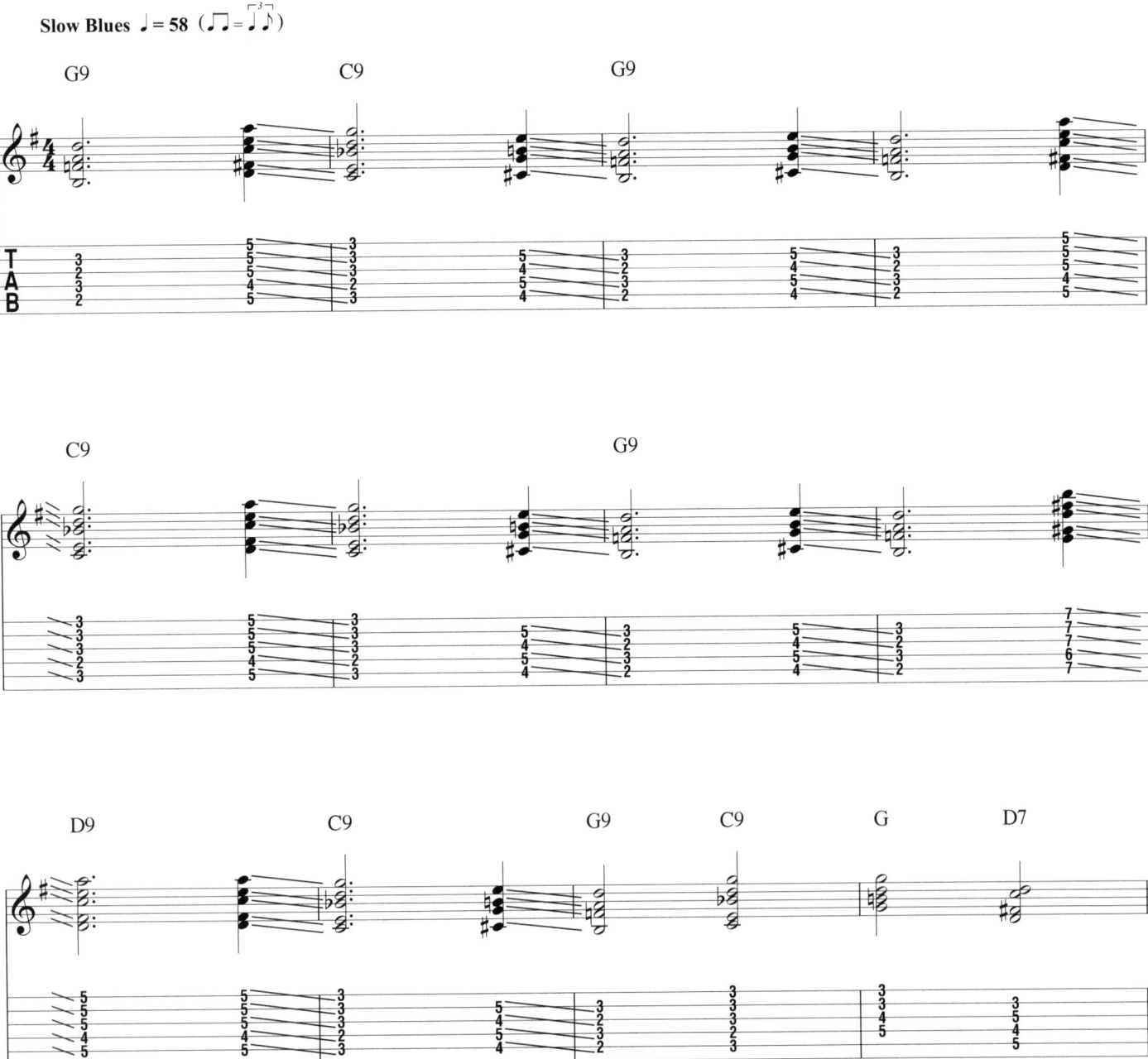

The Slow Blues Groove Solo

Here's a solo you can play over the Slow Blues jam track. This solo incorporates some new bend techniques, slides, and vibrato. The rhythm contains triplets and is a bit more complicated than the previous leads. Take your time and go through the solo riff by riff until you've got it down.

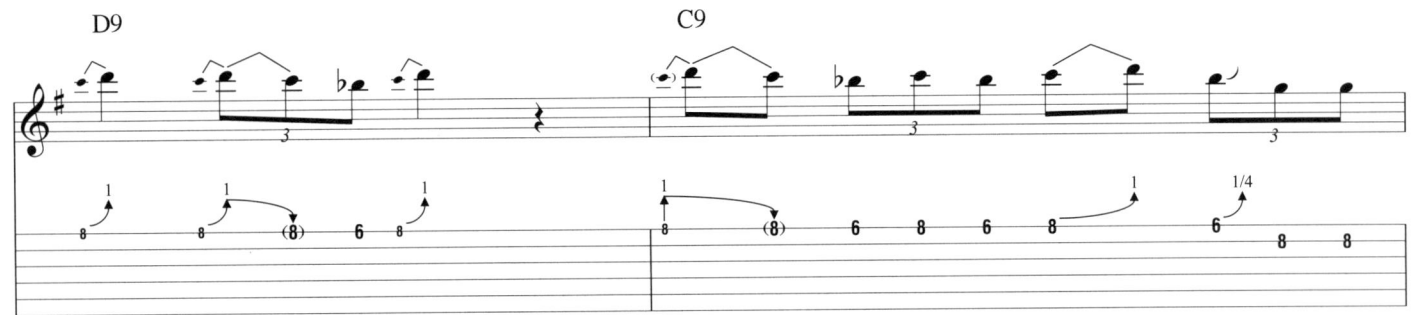

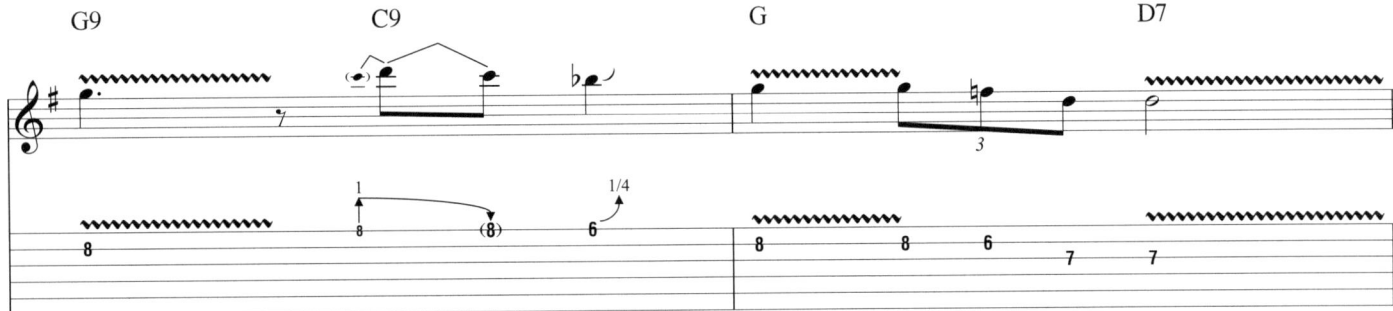

The Slow Blues Groove Solo II

Now let's create another solo to play over the Slow Blues jam track using a collage of riffs from the previous solos. The first section is from the Shuffle Blues Solo, followed by some riffs from the Rock 'n' Roll and Mojo Solos.

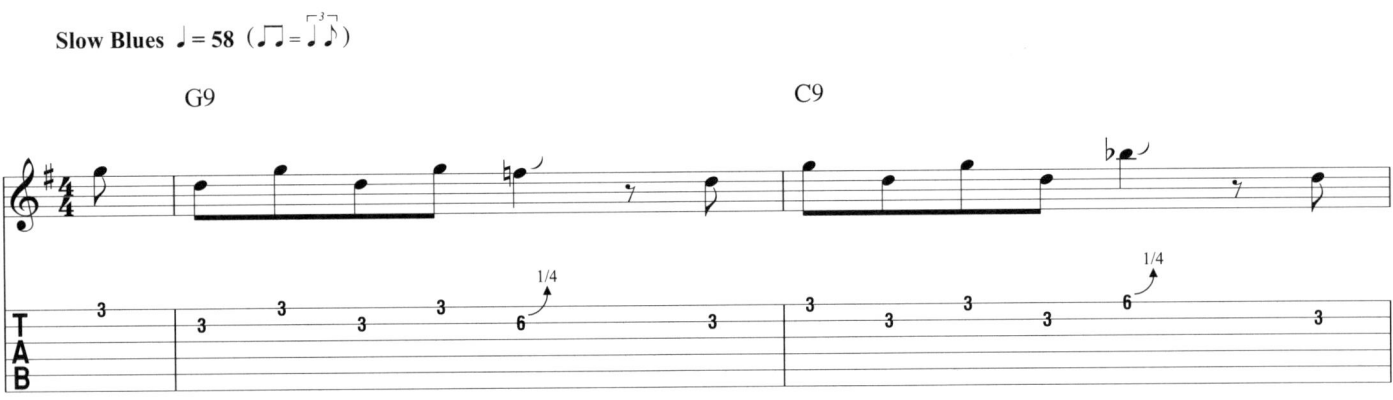

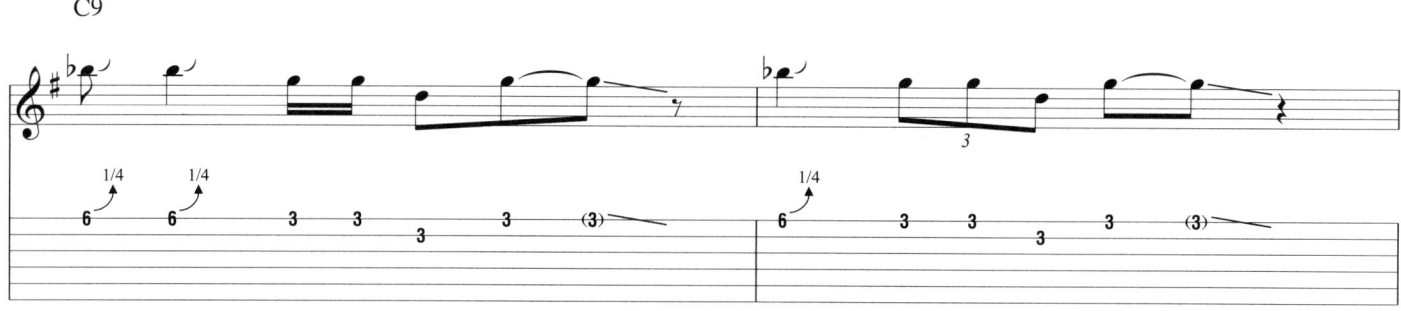

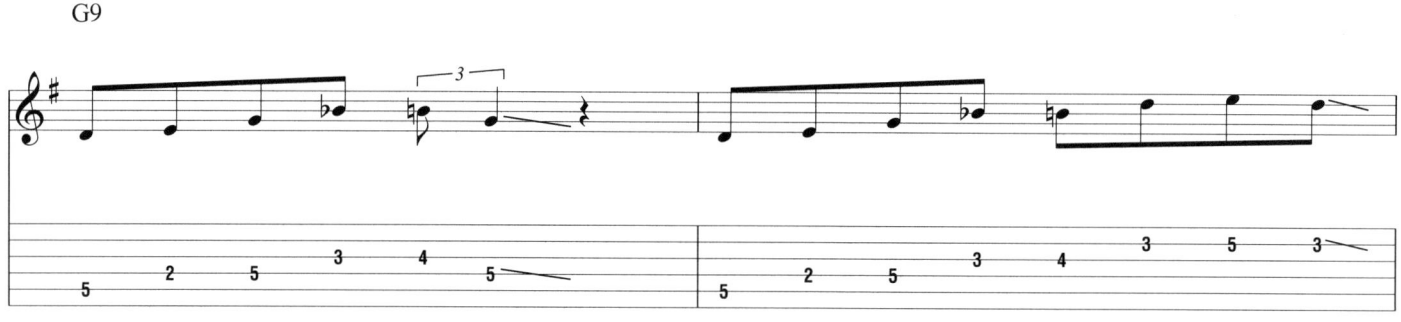

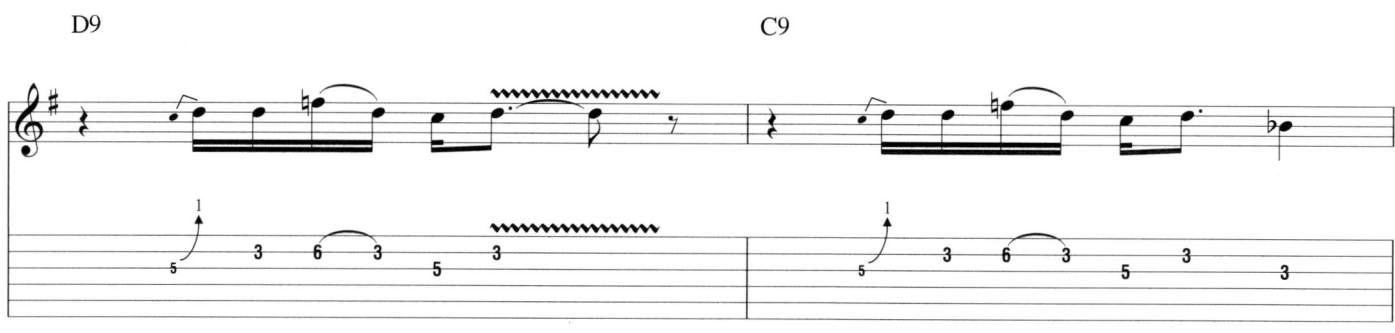

The Boogaloo Groove

The Boogaloo Groove Rhythm

The following Boogaloo Groove is an uptempo, driving rhythm in the key of E. It's a basic 12-bar blues using all seventh chords, followed by a repeated single-note bass figure in the second part of each measure. The chord progression is featured in its most basic form, without a quick change or turnaround.

The Boogaloo Groove Solo

Soloing in the key of E allows you to utilize the open strings. The first riff is an example of a unison double stop, incorporating the 5th fret E on the second string and the open first string to give the phrase more power. Throughout the rest of the solo, we've used the open strings to play various hammer-ons and pull-offs.

The Rock 'n' Roll and Mojo Solos Transposed to E

Now let's transpose a few of the previous solos and play them over the Boogaloo jam track. The riffs are essentially the same as before, but moving them to the key of E allows us to utilize more of the open strings.

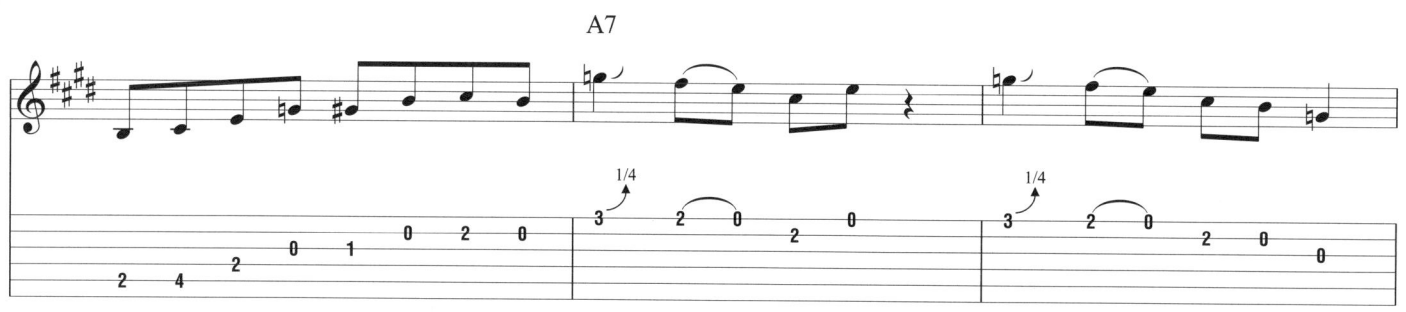

The Shuffle Solo Transposed to E

Transposing the shuffle solo to E also allows us to make great use of the open strings. Let the open 1st and 2nd strings in the main riff to ring out over each other to give it a cool banjo effect.

The Backwards Shuffle

The Backwards Shuffle Rhythm

This last groove is a shuffle rhythm with the emphasis on the upbeats; most of the downstrums are muted throughout. The progression is in the key of F and features a II-V chord change at measures 9 and 10. This is another common variation of the 12-bar blues that you'll encounter in many blues standards. Notice that we've also used the familiar quick change in the second measure, and in measure 7 we've switched positions and played the I chord (F7) at the 1st fret to set up the turnaround.

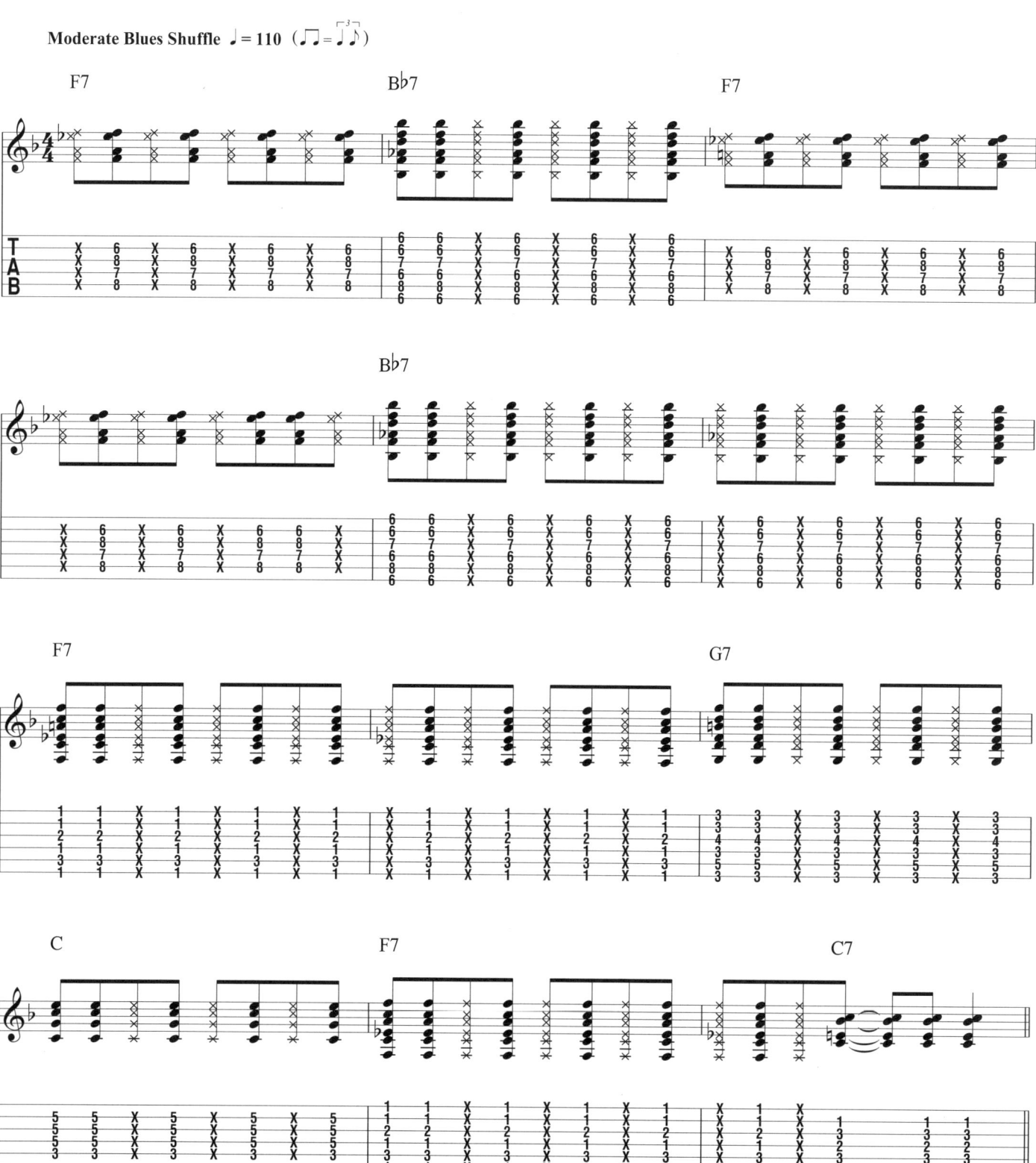

The Backwards Shuffle Solo

The first half of our final solo is a brand-new collection of riffs in the key of F. The second half is a collage of riffs from the previous chapters, all transposed to F. The solo starts off in the 1st position of the F minor pentatonic scale and switches over to the major pentatonic in the turnaround at measures 11 and 12. This leads into the second half of the solo which uses the major pentatonic riffs from the Mojo and Rock 'n' Roll solos.

Once you've gotten all of the leads in this program memorized and you have a good understanding of how to transpose the riffs to different keys, you can use them to create your own solos in any key. Get creative with the scales and come up with some new riffs to start building your own personal library of solos.

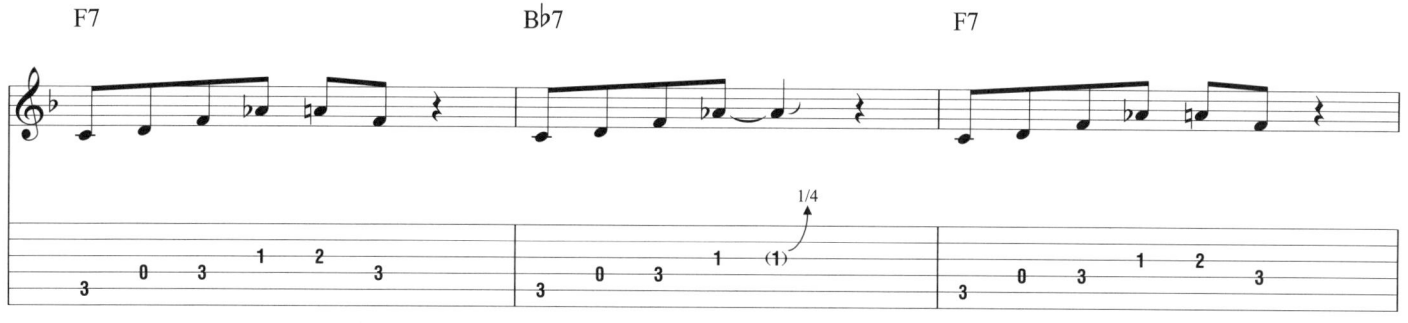

Great DVD selections from CHERRY LANE

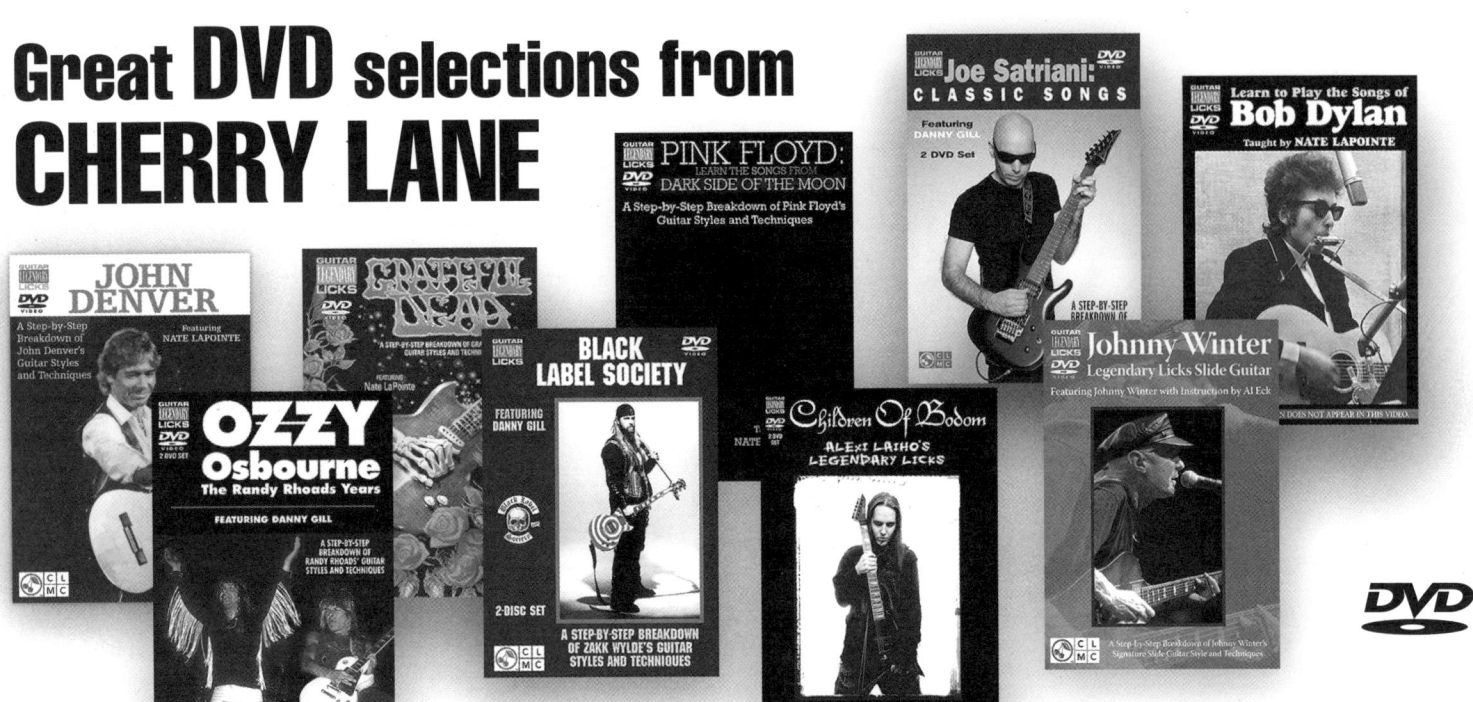

Steven Adler's Getting Started with Rock Drumming
taught by the Legendary Former Guns N' Roses Drummer!
02501387 DVD $29.99

Altered Tunings and Techniques for Modern Metal Guitar
taught by Rick Plunkett
02501457 DVD $19.99

Beginning Blues Guitar
RHYTHM AND SOLOS
taught by Al Ek
02501325 DVD $19.99

Black Label Society
featuring Danny Gill
Guitar Legendary Licks
02500983 2-DVD Set $29.95

Black Sabbath
featuring Danny Gill
Guitar Legendary Licks
02500874 DVD $24.95

Blues Masters by the Bar
taught by Dave Celentano
02501146 DVD $24.99

Children of Bodom
ALEXI LAIHO'S LEGENDARY LICKS
taught by Danny Gill
02501398 DVD $24.99

John Denver
featuring Nate LaPointe
Guitar Legendary Licks
02500917 DVD $24.95

Learn to Play the Songs of Bob Dylan
taught by Nate LaPointe
Guitar Legendary Licks
02500918 DVD $24.95

Funky Rhythm Guitar
taught by Buzz Feiten
02501393 DVD $24.99

Grateful Dead – Classic Songs
featuring Nate LaPointe
Guitar Legendary Licks
02500968 DVD $24.95

Grateful Dead
featuring Nate LaPointe
Guitar Legendary Licks
02500551 DVD $24.95

Guitar Heroes
taught by Danny Gill
Guitar Legendary Licks
02501069 2-DVD Set $29.95

The Latin Funk Connection
02501417 DVD $19.99

Metallica – 1983-1988
featuring Doug Boduch
Bass Legendary Licks
02500481 DVD $24.95

Metallica – 1988-1997
featuring Doug Boduch
Bass Legendary Licks
02500484 DVD $24.95

Metallica – 1983-1988
featuring Nathan Kilen
Drum Legendary Licks
02500482 DVD $24.95

Metallica – 1988-1997
featuring Nathan Kilen
Drum Legendary Licks
02500485 DVD $24.95

Metallica – 1983-1988
featuring Doug Boduch
Guitar Legendary Licks
02500479 DVD $24.95

Metallica – 1988-1997
featuring Doug Boduch
Guitar Legendary Licks
02500480 DVD $24.99

Mastering the Modes for the Rock Guitarist
taught by Dave Celentano
02501449 DVD $19.99

Home Recording Magazine's 100 Recording Tips and Tricks
STRATEGIES AND SOLUTIONS FOR YOUR HOME STUDIO
02500509 DVD $19.95

Ozzy Osbourne – The Randy Rhoads Years
featuring Danny Gill
Guitar Legendary Licks
02501301 2-DVD Set $29.99

Pink Floyd – Learn the Songs from Dark Side of the Moon
by Nate LaPointe
Guitar Legendary Licks
02500919 DVD $24.95

Rock Harmonica
taught by Al Ek
02501475 DVD $19.99

Poncho Sanchez
featuring the Poncho Sanchez Latin Jazz Band
02500729 DVD $24.95

Joe Satriani
featuring Danny Gill
Guitar Legendary Licks Series
02500767 2-DVD Set $29.95

Joe Satriani – Classic Songs
featuring Danny Gill
Guitar Legendary Licks
02500913 2-DVD Set $29.95

Johnny Winter
taught by Al Ek
Guitar Legendary Licks
02501307 2-DVD Set 29.99

Johnny Winter
SLIDE GUITAR
featuring Johnny Winter with instruction by Al Ek
Guitar Legendary Licks
02501042 DVD $29.95

Wolfmother
featuring Danny Gill
02501062 DVD $24.95

See your local music retailer or contact

EXCLUSIVELY DISTRIBUTED BY
HAL•LEONARD CORPORATION
7777 W. BLUEMOUND RD. P.O. BOX 13819 MILWAUKEE, WI 53213

Prices, contents, and availability subject to change without notice.